This book is dedicated to my mom, who taught me how to love. And to my family, who help me pass it on.

Good morning, friends!

Today is the day that I get to go on an adventure with my new friend! I was so excited, I could barely sleep last night!

I got ready for the day, ate a yummy breakfast, packed our lunch in my favorite picnic basket, and headed to The Butterfly Patch.

Just as I reached the garden gate, I spotted Toadstrom. I was so happy that he was already there, ready for our adventure!

I waved and called out in my happiest voice, "Good morning! Are you excited for our new adventure? I know I am!"

"Good morning," Toadstrom replied. "I was so excited, I could barely sleep last night! Where are we going today?"

"Today I thought we could go to Fairyfalls for a picnic," I said. "I packed nutrient sandwiches, wood chips, mud pies, and of course, water to wash it all down."

Toadstrom's eyes grew wide. "That sounds like a great idea!" He said with excitement.

We started down the path for Fairyfalls, both with a big smile on our face. Along the way, we took turns showing each other different flowers, leaves, and insects.

We laughed at silly things - like when I got tangled up in a spider web and jumped in surprise, or when Toadstrom tried to walk backward and almost tripped on a stick.

We were having so much fun, we started asking each other silly questions.

"If you had a superpower, what would you want it to be?" I asked.

"I would want the ability to heal people," Toadstrom replied.

I thought for a moment but before I could reply, Toadstrom gasped and pointed ahead. "We're here!!"

"Wow, it's so beautiful!" I exclaimed. "Now its time to pick the perfect spot for our picnic!"

"Look over there!" Toadstrom said. "It has the perfect view of Fairyfalls and plenty of space for our picnic!"

I couldn't believe my eyes, it really was the perfect spot. "I agree, let's get our picnic set up!" I said.

I laid out my checkered blanket, and we unpacked the picnic together.

First, we enjoyed our nutrient sandwiches. Then we decided the wood chips should be next - for a little crunch! We both said it at the same time, and we laughed.

For dessert, we saved the mudpies for last. We finished our picnic with the water. "We have to hydrate ourselves for our hike back to the garden," I said.

Before we headed back, we sat quietly and admired Fairyfalls for a little while longer. Toadstrom pointed to the waves crashing against the rocks.

"I think they look like clouds instead of water," he said. "I think they look like frogs sitting on the rocks at the bottom." I replied.

Toadstrom laughed, and together we started our walk back to The Butterfly Patch. The hike back was quiet - we were both feeling tired after such a big adventure.

When we reached The Butterfly Patch, we said goodnight and promised to meet again the next morning for another new adventure as friends!

I walked back to my hut, thinking about my favorite part of the day and how great the hike was.

When I finally curled up at home, I realized my favorite part of the adventure wasn't Fairyfalls at all.

It was having a friend to adventure with.

Goodnight, friends.

Check out my website for FREE coloring pages - just scan the code below!!

make your own mushroom

mushname: ______